Those Peculiar Pelicans

Sarah Cussen

Illustrated by Steve Weaver

Photographs by Roger Hammond

Pineapple Press, Inc.
Sarasota, Florida

Inquiries should be addressed to:

Pineapple Press, Inc.
P.O. Box 3889
Sarasota, Florida 34230

www.pineapplepress.com

Library of Congress Cataloging in Publication Data

Cussen, Sarah, 1980-
Those peculiar pelicans / Sarah Cussen ;
illustrated by Steve Weaver ;
photographs by Roger Hammond.-- 1st ed.
p. cm.
ISBN-13: 978-1-56164-340-0 (pbk. : alk. paper)
ISBN-10: 1-56164-340-8 (pbk. : alk. paper)
1. Pelicans--Miscellanea--Juvenile literature. I. Weaver, Steve, ill. II. Hammond, Roger, 1966- ill. III. Title.
QL696.P47C87 2005
598.4'3--dc22
2005012529

First Edition
10 9 8 7 6 5 4 3 2 1

Design by Steve Weaver
Printed in China

This one's for Max.

Contents

What kinds of pelicans will I see at the beach?

If you live in the American South, the pelicans you see down by the water are mostly Brown Pelicans. Brown Pelicans are the most common kind of pelican in the United States. Next time you go to the seashore, keep your eye out for these funny-looking brown birds with big beaks. You will find them sitting on the docks or hanging out near a fisherman, hoping for a free snack. Sometimes you might see an American White Pelican. The American White Pelican is more rare. They come to Florida for the winter from their homes in Canada and the northwestern United States.

How many kinds of pelicans are there?

There are 8 kinds, or species, of pelicans. These are the American White Pelican, the Australian Pelican, the Brown Pelican, the Dalmatian Pelican, the Eastern (or Great White) Pelican, the Peruvian Pelican, the Pink Backed Pelican, and the Spot Billed Pelican. The Dalmatian Pelican is the rarest. The Australian Pelican is the largest.

1 American White Pelican

2 Dalmatian Pelican

3 Pink Backed Pelican

4 Peruvian Pelican

5 Brown Pelican

6 Australian Pelican

7 Spot Billed Pelican

8 Eastern (or Great White) Pelican

○ American White Pelican   ○ Eastern (or Great White) Pelican
● Australian Pelican   ● Peruvian Pelican
○ Brown Pelican   ● Pink Backed Pelican
● Dalmation Pelican   ○ Spot Billed Pelican

Where in the world do pelicans live?

Pelicans live all over the world, on the ocean and by lakes.

Why are Brown Pelicans special?

Each species of pelican is interesting in its own way. The male Brown Pelican attracts a mate by taking the female a stick or a feather. If she accepts the gift, she is accepting the male bird as her mate.

How do pelicans hunt for food?

The Brown Pelican dives from the air and uses its beak and the pouch under its beak as a net to catch small fish. When other lazy pelicans see one diving, they join in. That way they don't have to go looking for other fish. American White Pelicans have a different way to fish. They swim in a line or form a circle and herd the fish into shallow water.

How do Brown Pelicans dive-bomb fish?

The Brown Pelican plunges from up to 60 feet, bill-first into the water. That's twice as high as the highest diver in the Olympics! Hitting the water like that would kill most birds, but not the pelican. A pelican has small air sacs to cushion the fall. It can go on to enjoy its dinner.

How much can pelicans fit in their beaks?

Pelicans have amazing beaks. They fill them with huge gulps of water from the sea. Then they let the water dribble out and they eat the fish that are left. The skin on the bottom part of the bill is very loose and can expand. The pelican can hold nearly 3 gallons of water in its mouth. Can you picture pouring 3 gallons of water into your mouth? The Australian Pelican has the longest beak of any bird in the world: 15 to 20 inches long. That's probably longer than your arm!

Do pelicans steal fish from fishermen?

Some fishermen think that pelicans steal the fish that they want to catch. These fishermen are wrong! It's true that pelicans do follow fishing boats and hang out at piers looking for handouts, but when pelicans hunt they never catch the same fish as human fishermen. The three pelicans in the photo are begging. They are so cute it's hard to refuse!

But no one should give them handouts. They are wild birds and they must not become dependent on humans.

Do other birds steal fish from pelicans?

While the Brown Pelican is draining the water from its bill after a dive, gulls often try to catch the tiny fish that escape. A gull will sometimes even perch on the pelican's head and reach into the bill. Can you picture someone sitting on your head and picking up your crumbs?

How much do pelicans eat?

Every day an adult pelican needs to eat about 4 pounds of fish. This weighs about as much 8 Big Macs®! Pelican parents feed their babies for about 13 weeks until the babies can catch their own fish. During this time, each baby bird will eat about 150 pounds of fish. That's a lot of food for the parents to carry home!

How big are pelican wings?

If you measure a Brown Pelican from one end of its wings to the other, it is 6½ to 7½ feet. That's as long as the tallest basketball star is tall! The largest American White Pelicans have wings of up to 9 feet.

If a basketball star were that tall, he would never have to jump!

How high can a pelican fly?

The Brown Pelicans you see at the beach like to spend much of their time near the ground. But American White Pelicans like to soar high in the clouds. They catch rides on the wind and go very high. These huge birds may look funny on the ground, but they fly like graceful ballerinas up to heights of thousands of feet. Imagine flying in a plane and passing by a pelican!

How tall are pelicans?

Pelicans are big birds. Brown Pelicans are 2 - 2½ feet tall. American White Pelicans are even larger. They are 3 -3½ feet tall. If you measure from end of beak to end of tail, the Browns are almost 4 feet long.

How many eggs does a pelican lay?

Pelicans lay 2 or 3 eggs. Both the mother and the father take care of the eggs. They keep the eggs warm underneath them, which is where the other egg is in this picture.

What do baby pelicans look like?

When they first hatch, pelicans, like many other birds, have no feathers. They look scrawny and are very hungry and demand food constantly so they can eat and grow.

Their first feathers are all white. Baby pelicans stay in or near the nest until they are about 3 months old. The one shown on the towel was rescued and grew up at a bird sanctuary. Then he flew away on his own.

Where do pelicans make their nests?

Brown Pelicans roost in trees, often on small islands. A rookery is where lots of them live together. Pelicans love company! They are very happy in big groups, or flocks. This makes it easier to protect themselves from other animals. Animals like raccoons try to eat their eggs. The pelicans can warn each other of danger when they live together. Up to almost 2000 pelicans have been seen living together. That's a big family!

How do pelicans stay cool?

Pelicans don't just use their beaks to catch fish. They also use them as an air conditioner! When it gets very hot, a pelican stretches out its pouch and moves it around. There is lots of blood flowing through a pelican's neck. The air cools the blood and this cools off the whole pelican.

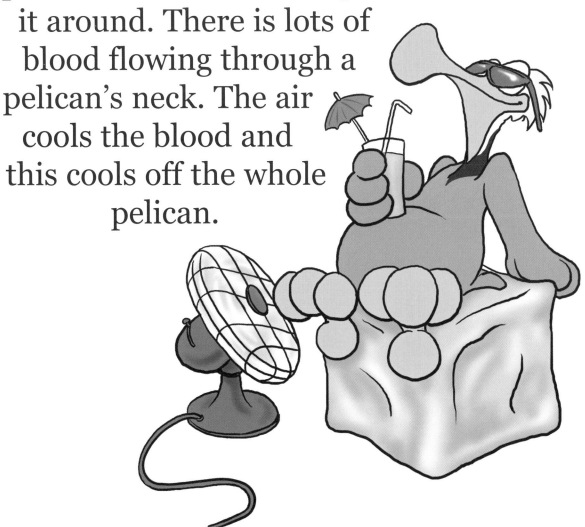

What are the dangers to pelicans?

People are the biggest danger to pelicans. People sometimes put poison on their plants to keep the bugs away. But this poison can hurt other animals as well. Some years ago, a poison called DDT was hurting the eggs of pelicans. But this story has a happy ending. People were not allowed to use DDT anymore. Pelican eggs began to hatch again.

Pelicans also get caught on fish hooks and get tangled in fishing lines. This is very dangerous for them. There are bird rescuers in many coastal areas who help tangled and injured birds.

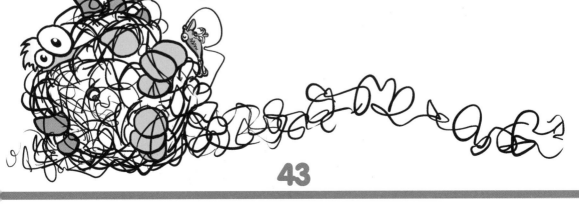

Why do some Brown Pelicans look different from others?

Until they are three years old, Brown Pelicans are brown all over, except for a white belly. The beak is gray with a yellowish hook at the end.

Adult pelicans are dark gray-brown. The head and neck are white. At breeding time, the top of the head turns yellow, and part of the neck becomes dark chocolate-brown.

Males and females look alike except that the male is a little bit bigger and has a longer beak.

Who are the pelican's ancestors?

Pelicans are descendants of an ancient group of sea birds that lived about 100 million years ago. This was when huge dinosaurs like the Tyrannosaurus and the Triceratops roamed the earth. There were even flying dinosaurs called Pterosaurs. Can you picture an ancient pelican flying over the head of the T-Rex?

Origami Pelican

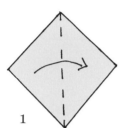

1

Fold in half.

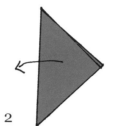

2

Unfold.

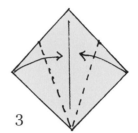

3

Fold to the center.

4

5

Turn over.

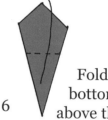

6

Fold the
bottom tip
above the top.

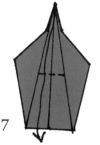

7

Fold point down.

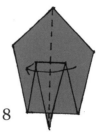

8

Fold in half side to side.

9

Pull out the neck
and head. (Pinch
top of head.)

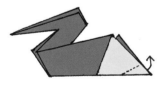

10

Fold the tail up
into the middle
by bending in
and pinching.

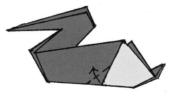

11

Fold up wingtips on
both sides.

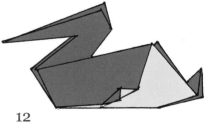

12

Pelican

Activities

Make an Origami Pelican

Origami is the Japanese name for the art of paper folding. You can use any kind of square paper, including construction paper or white paper (cut into a square). Construction paper is thicker and doesn't fold as well as thinner paper. The best results come from origami paper, which has a different color on each side.You can find it in craft shops or you can order it at many sites online.

Tip: If your pelican won't sit properly,
you can glue its wingtips to a paper base.

Make a Collage Pelican

Collage comes from the French word for glue. To make a collage, you glue different things to a surface to make a picture or design. You can use all sorts of things to glue onto this pelican outline to make your very own collage. You can go outside and find sticks, leaves, little stones, maybe even feathers. And you can add bits of colored paper or little pieces cut from magazines.
Let your imagination be your guide!

Here is a pelican outline for you to use.
(You can make it bigger with a photocopy machine.)

Here is a sample collage pelican made with bits of paper (construction paper and magazines).

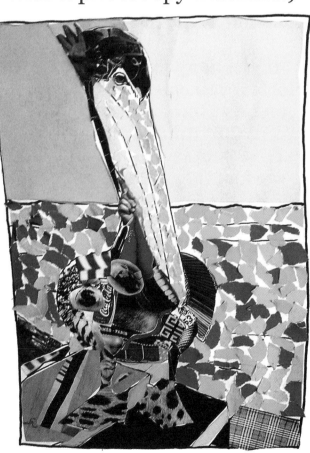

About Pelican Man's Bird Sanctuary

The Pelican Man's Bird Sanctuary in Sarasota is Florida's largest Wildlife Rescue and Rehabilitation Center, rescuing over five thousand sick, injured, and orphaned birds each year.

All the patients are treated in the Sanctuary's hospital and the aim is to rehabilitate the bird and return it back to the wild. If release is not possible because it could not survive in the wild, the bird will be given a home in a spacious, natural habitat at the Sanctuary. Many pelicans are living there.

If you happen to be near Sarasota on the west coast of Florida, you can visit Pelican Man's Bird Sanctuary, located on City Island. It is open to visitors 10 A.M. to 5 P.M. daily (except Christmas and Thanksgiving). Their phone number is 941-388-4444. You can learn more about pelicans and the work of the Sanctuary by visiting www.pelicanman.org.

If you find an injured bird, please call your nearest wildlife rehabilitator. You can find one near you by going to the website of the National Wildlife Rehabilitators Association http://www.nwrawildlife.org/home.asp.

Where to Learn More about Pelicans

Some books about pelicans:

Keiser, Frances, and Hugh Keiser (Illustrator). The
Adventures of Pelican Pete: A Bird
is Born. Sagaponack Books, 1999. (ages 4-8)

Patent, Dorothy Hinshaw, and William Munoz. Brown
Pelicans (Early Bird Nature Books). Lerner Publications,
2005. (ages 4-8)

Taylor, Bonnie Highsmith. Mattie: A Brown Pelican (Cover-
to-Cover Chapter Books:
Animal Adv.-Air). Perfection Learning, 2001. (ages 4-8)

Some good pelican websites:

www.pelicanman.org
(Learn more about pelican rescue. Also includes frequently
asked questions about pelicans)

http://www.mangoverde.com/birdsound/fam/fam15.html
(A selection of photos, videos, and recordings
of the world's pelicans)

http://endangered.fws.gov/i/b/sab2s.html
(Information from the US Fish and Wildlife Service)

About the Author

Sarah Cussen grew up in Sarasota, Florida, and returns frequently to enjoy the weather and the wildlife, especially the pelicans. She now lives and works in London and visits the pelicans at the London Zoo.

If you enjoyed reading this book, here are some other Pineapple Press titles you might enjoy as well. To request our complete catalog or to place an order, write to Pineapple Press, P.O. Box 3889, Sarasota, Florida 34230, or call 1-800-PINEAPL (746-3275). Or visit our website at www.pineapplepress.com.

Those Funny Flamingos by Jan Lee Wicker. Illustrated by Steve Weaver. This is the first of the "Those Funny" series. Learn why those funny flamingos are pink, stand on one leg, eat upside down, and much more. Ages 5-9.

Drawing Florida Wildlife by Frank Lohan. The clearest, easiest method yet for learning to draw Florida's birds, reptiles, amphibians, and mammals. All ages.

Dinosaurs of the South by Judy Cutchins and Ginny Johnston. Dinosaurs lived in the southeastern United States. Loaded with full-color fossil photos as well as art to show what the dinos might have looked like. Ages 8-12.

Ice Age Giants of the South by Judy Cutchins and Ginny Johnston. Learn about the huge animals and reptiles that lived here during the Ice Age. Meet saber-toothed cats, dire wolves, mammoths, giant sloths, and more. Ages 8-12.

Giant Predators of the Ancient Seas by Judy Cutchins and Ginny Johnston. Meet the giant creatures that prowled the waters of prehistory. Ages 8-12.

Florida A to Z by Susan Jane Ryan. Illustrated by Carol Tornatore. From Alligator to Zephyrhills, you'll find out more about Florida packed in this alphabet than you can imagine-200 facts and pictures on Florida history, geography, nature, and people. Ages 8-12.

Florida Lighthouses for Kids by Elinor De Wire. Learn why some lighthouses are tall and some short, why a cat parachuted off St. Augustine Lighthouse, where Florida skeleton and spider lighthouses stand, and much more. Lots of color pictures. Ages 9 and up.

The Young Naturalist's Guide to Florida by Peggy Lantz and Wendy Hale. Where and how to look for Florida's most interesting creatures, including in Florida's special places like the Everglades, coral reefs, sinkholes, salt marshes, and beaches. Ages 10-14.

The Florida Water Story by Peggy Lantz and Wendy Hale. Learn about Florida's water systems-from raindrops to the sea and the many plants and animals that depend on them. Ages 9 up.